The PORTABLE Father

Stacey Granger

Cumberland House

Nashville, Tennessee

Published by Cumberland House Publishing, Inc.,
2200 Abbott Martin Road, Suite 102, Nashville, Tennessee 37215

Distributed to the trade by Andrews and McMeel, 4520 Main
Street, Kansas City, Missouri 64111.

Design by Bruce Gore, Gore Studio, Inc., Nashville, Tennessee.
Illustrations by Wes Ware.

Library of Congress Cataloging-in-Publication Data

Granger, Stacey, A., 1969-
The portable fother / Stacey Granger.
p. cm.
ISBN 1-888952-42-3 (alk. paper)
1. Fathers—Quotations, maxims, etc. 2. Fatherhood—
Quotations, maxims, etc. 3. Fathers—Humor. I. Title.
PN6084.F3G73 1997
306.874'2—dc21 96-50996
CIP

Printed in the United States of America
1 2 3 4 5 6 7 8—01 00 99 98 97

To Dad

who encouraged me
when my dreams seemed
too high to reach

To Walt

whose love and support
have kept the dreams alive

Introduction

THERE ISN'T A DAY THAT GOES BY THAT I DON'T FEEL the impact my father has had on my life. Dad was the one who always said, "There are three types of people in this world: Those who make things happen; those who watch things happen; and those who sit around wondering 'What happened?'" He also said it was up to me which type of person I became.

Fathers are the ones who are full of old clichés that, to a child, make no sense whatsoever. My father used to say, "The more things change, the more they stay the same." My brother, sister, and I swore he said that only to shut us up and give us something to think about.

In a traditional family, I feel that fathers get the short end of the stick in the time spent with their children, insomuch as they are spending most of their time working to pay for having them. And as we all know, "There are only so many hours in a day." But fathers seem to make up for their absence by trying to make every minute spent with their children count by teaching them the finer things of life.

For instance, while I've spent years trying to teach my son how to behave like a perfect little gentleman, his father took less than five minutes to show him how to make disgusting sounds with his armpit and hand—two objects he takes with him wherever he goes (to church, for instance).

I remember so well being a child and how the day seemed to stretch on forever, until the sound I'd been waiting for sounded in the driveway. That old familiar car would pull in and an undefinable excitement would overwhelm me as my brother, sister, and I would rush for the door yelling, "Dad's home! Dad's home!"

My father always seemed to be the biggest and most wonderful person in my life. And even if I didn't understand everything he said to me back then, I was happy to have just a little piece of his time, and those things did start to make more sense as I got older and heard my husband saying those same things to our children.

And at five o'clock at our house, when that old familiar car pulls in the drive, the sound usually muffled out by the gleeful chorus of our children calling, "Dad's home!", the thing that most readily comes to my mind is: The more things change the more they stay the same.

-Stacey Granger

The PORTABLE Father

Go ask your mother.

Do I look like a money tree?

Listen to your mother.

Hey, little buddy, give me "five."

Don't let your mother see you with that. She'll have my hide.

When you are all grown up, you can decide what's best for you.

Close that door!
You think we can afford
to heat the outside?

Turn off the lights!
We don't own stock in
the electric company.

Don't make a mountain out of a molehill.

What do you mean, you had a little accident with the car?

I'll help you when I get home from work.

You think your life is tough now. Just wait until you have to go out and earn a living.

I wouldn't use that bathroom for a while if I were you.

When you see the door closed, knock before you enter.

I don't need any instructions to put it together. Just hand me my hammer.

Where did you put those instructions?

See? You take the worm, and you put it on the hook.

Don't ever try to pull a stunt like that again!

We can't always have everything we want in this life.

And what did your mother have to say about this?

If you don't shape up, you may never live long enough to grow up.

Let me tell you a thing or two.

If it's not yours, don't touch it.

Don't judge a book by its cover

I want you in before midnight.

Let's surprise Mommy.

Do you have enough money?

I just walked in the door.

I had a long day.

◈

Where's my newspaper?

◈

We'll do it on Saturday.

How does Mom do this?

If you know what's good for you…

Listen up. I'm only going to say this once.

I am your father, so what I say goes.

Let's not tell your mother about this.

Who wants to go out for ice cream?

A bird in the hand is worth two in the bush.

If you do the work, you'll reap the rewards.

What am I, MasterCard?

When did you get so big?

Say "Uncle!"

Let me show you how it works.

Straight from the mouths of babes.

Let's play "Who can be the quietest."

At the end of the day, I'm tired.

Give me a chance to think about it.

As long as you clean it up when you're finished.

Start cleaning up. Your mom's on her way home.

It doesn't matter if you win or lose. It's how you play the game.

Cheaters never win. But if you do cheat, don't get caught.

I'll help you down this time, but next time don't climb up so high.

Everything happens for a reason.

Learn from your mistakes.

Things have a way of working out.

Don't put off until tomorrow what you can do today.

You'll be more of a help by not trying to help.

Just don't kill each other before your mother gets home.

Where does Mommy keep the aspirin?

Don't sweat the small stuff.

Let's not start this again.

Well, would you look at that!

I don't have the energy for all this bickering.

It's just a little bug. It won't hurt you.

Maybe tomorrow.

Just one more time,
and then that's it.

Now, wait just a minute!

How could I possibly say no when you ask me like that?

Don't give up so easily. It's not over until the fat lady sings.

Keep your cotton-pickin' hands off my stuff.

What do you mean you couldn't find it?

My little girl is going out with a boy?

Why is it I'm always the last to know?

Since when are you old enough to start dating?

You win some, you lose some.

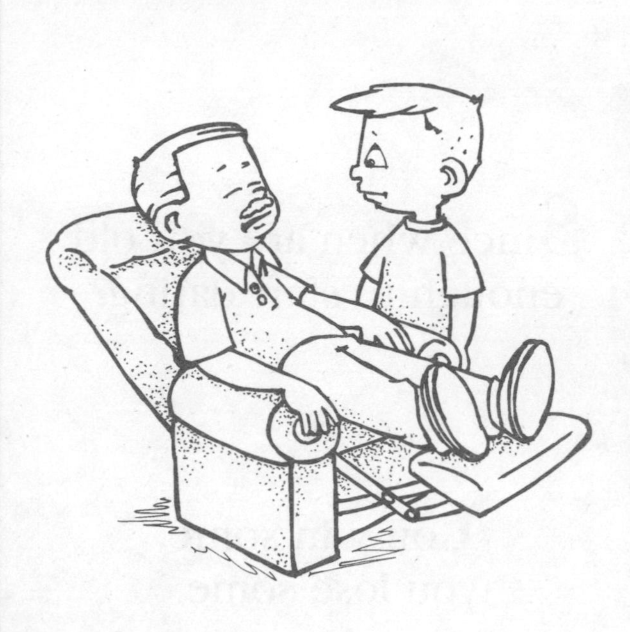

Dad just needs to close his eyes
and rest for a minute.

Did I ever tell you how far I had to walk to school?

Use your fists as the last resort.

Like it, or lump it.

Do you see this belt?

Life is a chance.

Can't you see I'm busy?

◈

Close, but no cigar.

◈

You reap what you sow.

Doesn't anything I say hold any weight around here?

If you're going to play with fire, you're going to get burned.

I know you don't want me to come in there!

You know what your grandfather would have said if I had tried that?

Righty tighty. Lefty loosey.

I suppose I'll have to wait till the snow thaws to find my screwdriver.

If you borrow something of mine, put it back where you got it.

While I'm away, son, you'll be the man of the house.

If you can't stand the heat, get out of the kitchen.

Don't leave your bike behind the car.

Put it on my workbench. I'll see if I can fix it.

I'm watching! I'm watching!

Why did you ask, if you were going to do it anyway?

Let me recharge my batteries.

My life does not revolve around you.

Who gave you permission to do that?

Waste not, want not.

Life isn't always a bed of roses.

Stick to your guns.

When you pay the bills, you can make the rules.

I know it doesn't taste like Mom makes it, but eat it anyway.

A lot of kids would die to be in your shoes.

Respect the wishes of others.

Why do boys call here at all hours of the night?

I know you think I'm stupid, but the older you get, the smarter I'll seem.

Ask your grandfather.
He thinks he knows
everything.

Take it up
with your mother.
She's the boss.

You got me a new tie? How'd you know I needed one?

What's the magic word?

◈

You're asking for it.

◈

What's the big idea of this?

Don't you have a shorter book you'd like me to read you?

How come I pay the phone bill but never get to use the phone?

If you act like a daredevil, you're going to pick up a few scrapes.

You didn't listen to me, and now you want me to feel sorry for you?

Furniture is made to be sat on, not bounced on.

Come on, a little rain won't melt you.

Put it on your Christmas list.

It can't be as bad as all that.

Help Daddy take off his boots.

I told you not to do that.

Not in this lifetime,
you won't!

Over my dead body!

Does anybody care what I think?

No, I'm not lost. I know exactly where we are.

Trouble seems to be your middle name.

The time for talk has passed.

I want to see you hitting the books more and bringing up those grades.

You'd better get crackin'.

What would your mother say if she saw you doing that?

Yes, this family is a democracy, but I'm the president.

You and the dog are going for a walk.

I only want you to be happy.

What did you do to your hair?

Next time maybe you'll know better.

All right, that's the third time you've told me I'm the world's greatest dad.

I'm still waiting for the other shoe to drop.

You can't learn to swim if you don't get in the water.

How much is this going to cost me?

Pull my finger.

I've got everything under control.

If I want something done right around here, I guess I'll have to do it myself.

You kids are eating me out of house and home.

It's about time you started pulling your own weight.

Don't get lippy with me, young man!

I'm still your father.

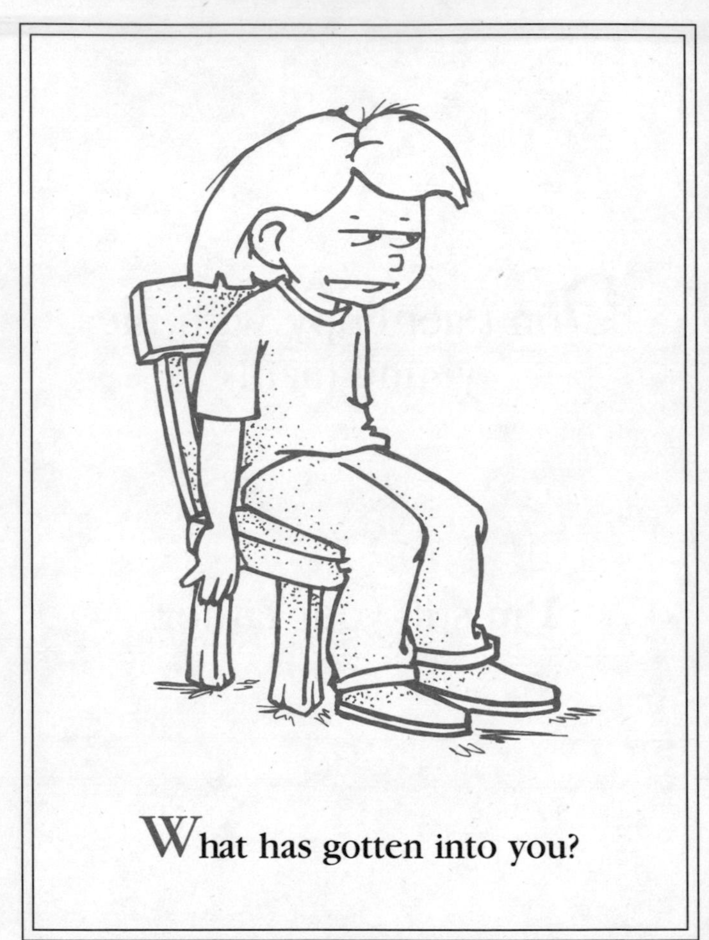

What has gotten into you?

Some day you'll
look back on all of this
and laugh.

If you can't
run with the big dogs,
stay on the porch.

I've got enough on my mind without you adding to it.

Take responsibility for your own actions.

I'll help you just as soon as the game is over.

If you lose, lose graciously.

Keep both hands on the wheel.

A penny saved is a penny earned.

The more things change, the more they stay the same.

If you abuse your privileges, I may be forced to take some away.

All right, who put the ding in the car door?

Take that kind of play outside.

If you think you're going to get away with that, you've got another think coming.

If you're bored, go find something to do.

If you can't find something to occupy your time, I can always put you to work.

There are too many chiefs in this family and not enough Indians.

If you lie down with dogs, you're going to get up with fleas.

A rolling stone gathers no moss.

One man's trash is another man's treasure.

Someday when you're rich and famous, don't forget your dear old dad.

One more game on that computer, and your mind will turn to mush.

Choke up on the bat.

Step into your swing.

Watch the ball until it hits your glove.

Keep your eye on the ball.

If the shoe fits,
wear it.

You made your bed.
Now you must lie
in it.

The more you know, the farther you'll go.

Close only counts in horseshoes and hand grenades.

All's fair in love and war.

Never go to sleep with an argument unsettled.

Treat people as you would have them treat you.

An apple a day keeps the doctor away.

Don't fill up on junk food.

Don't disappoint me.

Watch your mouth.

Cut that out!

In a few years, this will all be water under the bridge.

The squeaky wheel gets the grease.

Make sure what you say is true, and no one will ever doubt your word.

Trust is hard to mend once it's broken.

Keep your chin up.

He who hesitates is lost.

Do as I say, not as I do.

The truth hurts, doesn't it?

Don't burn your bridges.

It's a dog-eat-dog world.

How come my tools keep disappearing out of my toolbox?

My screwdriver is not meant to dig holes in the yard.

God gave you a brain. Try using it, for a change.

People who live in glass houses shouldn't throw stones.

I'm only telling you this for your own good.

The early bird gets the worm.

Where there's a will, there's a way.

I want to know where you've been, what you've been doing, and who you've been doing it with.

I wasn't born yesterday, you know.

I think it's
about time you started
thinking about your
future.

A fool and his money
are soon parted.

You have to be real quiet, or you'll scare the fish away.

Sometimes you seem to be your own worst enemy.

When you earn the money, you'll appreciate it more.

I don't care what your watch says, the clock on the wall here at home says midnight.

When I used to do something like that, your Granddad would say, "Whasamatawiyou?"

As long as
you try your hardest,
that's all I'll ask
of you.

If you can't remember it,
it must have not been all
that important in the
first place.

I'll give you a dollar if you change the baby's diaper.

If you ever want to get a good job, you'll have to finish school.

If you want something bad enough, don't ever give up.

I hope I didn't hear you say what I think I heard you say.

You can't stuff so much in the toilet and still expect it to flush.

Just who do you think you are?

Just who do you think you’re talking to?

Just where do you think you’rc going?

If you'd try as hard to get your homework done as you do making up excuses, you'd have straight A's.

How do you expect to graduate with grades like these?

Oh, you want your ears pierced? I'll go get my tools and pierce them for you.

Next time you try a stunt like that, heads are going to roll!

I'm going to ground you until you're thirty.

Honey, look what *your* son just got into!

What would I do without you, Princess?

I'll always be here for you to confide in.

If you don't like the way I drive, you can get out and walk.

Beggars can't be choosers.

Bite your tongue.

It's the thought that counts.

The day you were born was the happiest day of my life.

God gave you two ears and one mouth. So listen twice as much as you talk.

Look, I found this quarter behind your ear.

Use your head for something besides a hat rack.

You did great, son.

That umpire was blind.

Zip your pants.

That's for the birds!

Hold your horses.

Well, for Pete's sake!

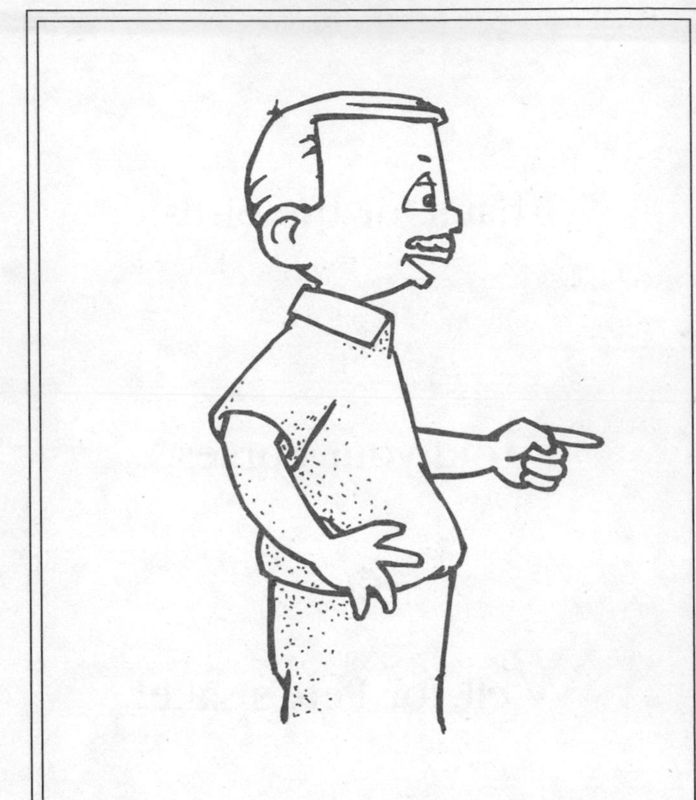

Do you think I like getting mad?

Kill 'em with kindness,
I always say.

Don't judge a man
until you've walked a mile
in his shoes.

You're getting too heavy for me to give pony rides.

You've got way too many toys already.

They don't make 'em like they used to.

Who left this dump truck on the stairs?

Don't take a lazy man's load.

Have you got rocks in your head?

All right, I'm gonna count to three…

You get that temper from your mom's side of the family.

I know spiders look scary, but they help us by eating bugs.

Smile.

Good things come to those who wait.

Stop pestering your sister.

Honey, what did we get Junior for his birthday?

If all of your friends were jumping off a bridge, would you jump, too?

If I had behaved like that, my father would have taken me behind the woodshed.

If I talked to my father the way you talk to me…

I'm not going to ask you again.

What's going on in here?

You're cruisin' for a bruisin'.

You're itchin' for a switchin'.

No son of mine is going out looking like that.

Move out of the way of the TV. You're not a window.

You want to tell me what's in this report card before I open it?

Smoking will stunt your growth.

Teeth are for eating, not for cracking nuts.

Quiet! I'm watching the game.

Of course I'm not sick. Dads never get sick.

I hope you're satisfied!

Because you didn't pay me back the last twenty-seven times.

Anything worth doing is worth doing well.

It'll feel better when it quits hurting.

Don't throw that away. We might need it someday.

Don't you have something you want to tell me?

Don't make me tell you again, young man.

Eat those Brussels sprouts. They'll put hair on your chest.

I don't take the trash out anymore. That's what I have you kids for.

You can't get blood from a turnip.

Please don't use your shirt as a napkin.

If you can't say anything nice, don't say anything at all.

You'd argue with a fence post.

What goes around, comes around.

Another day, another dollar.

You'll always be Daddy's little girl.

You make me so proud to be your father.

I love you.

ISBN 1-888952-30-X